The Positivity Project: Nurturing Growth and Success in Every Aspect of Life

Sakshi Patel

Copyright © [2023]

Title: The Positivity Project: Nurturing Growth and Success in Every Aspect of Life

Author's: Sakshi Patel.

All rights reserved. No part of this publication may be reproduced, stored in a retrieval system, or transmitted in any form or by any means, electronic, mechanical, photocopying, recording, or otherwise, without the prior written permission of the publisher or author, except in the case of brief quotations embodied in critical reviews and certain other non-commercial uses permitted by copyright law.

This book was printed and published by [Publisher's: Sakshi Patel] in [2023]

ISBN:

TABLE OF CONTENTS

Chapter 1: The Power of Positive Thinking — 06

Introduction to Positive Thinking

Understanding the Mind-Body Connection

Benefits of Positive Thinking

Overcoming Negative Thought Patterns

Chapter 2: Cultivating a Positive Mindset — 14

Recognizing and Challenging Negative Self-Talk

Practicing Gratitude and Appreciation

Embracing Optimism and Hope

Developing Resilience in the Face of Challenges

Chapter 3: Building Positive Relationships — 22

The Importance of Healthy Connections

Enhancing Communication and Active Listening Skills

Nurturing Empathy and Compassion

Resolving Conflict Positively

Chapter 4: Achieving Personal Growth and Success   30

Setting Goals and Visualizing Success

Harnessing the Power of Self-Discipline and Motivation

Embracing Failure as a Stepping Stone to Success

Cultivating a Growth Mindset for Continuous Improvement

Chapter 5: Fostering Positive Habits and Routines   38

Establishing a Morning Routine for a Productive Day

Incorporating Mindfulness and Meditation Practices

Prioritizing Self-Care and Wellbeing

Creating a Positive Environment for Success

Chapter 6: Spreading Positivity in the World   46

The Ripple Effect of Positive Actions

Acts of Kindness and Generosity

Promoting Social Connection and Community Engagement

Inspiring Others to Embrace Positivity

Chapter 7: Overcoming Obstacles to Positivity 54

Identifying and Managing Stress

Overcoming Self-Doubt and Fear

Dealing with Criticism and Negativity

Maintaining Positivity in Challenging Situations

Chapter 8: Sustaining Positivity for Long-Term Growth 62

Creating Personal Affirmations and Mantras

Building a Supportive Network

Practicing Self-Reflection and Self-Celebration

Embracing a Lifetime Commitment to Positivity

Conclusion: The Journey to Nurturing Growth and Success 70

Chapter 1: The Power of Positive Thinking

Introduction to Positive Thinking

Welcome to the subchapter on "Introduction to Positive Thinking" from the book "The Positivity Project: Nurturing Growth and Success in Every Aspect of Life." This chapter is dedicated to everyone who seeks to transform their lives by harnessing the power of positive thinking. Whether you are a student, a professional, a parent, or simply someone looking to find more joy and fulfillment, this subchapter is for you.

Positive thinking is not just a passing trend or a temporary state of mind. It is a powerful mindset that can shape your entire outlook on life and profoundly impact your well-being. The practice of positive thinking involves consciously choosing to focus on the positive aspects of your experiences, thoughts, and emotions, and looking for opportunities for growth and gratitude.

The concept of positive thinking is rooted in the belief that our thoughts have a direct influence on our emotions and actions. When we think positively, we open ourselves up to possibilities, solutions, and happiness. Positive thinking empowers us to approach challenges with resilience, to see setbacks as learning opportunities, and to cultivate a sense of gratitude for the blessings in our lives.

In this subchapter, we will explore the benefits of positive thinking and how it can enhance various aspects of your life. We will delve into the science behind positive thinking, examining how it affects our brain, emotions, and overall well-being. You will learn practical techniques and strategies to cultivate a positive mindset, including mindfulness, gratitude practices, and affirmations.

Moreover, we will address common misconceptions about positive thinking and debunk the notion that it is simply a form of wishful thinking or ignoring the realities of life. Positive thinking is not about denying negative emotions or suppressing challenges. It is about acknowledging and accepting them while choosing to focus on finding solutions and maintaining an optimistic perspective.

Throughout this subchapter, you will find inspiring stories of individuals who have transformed their lives through the power of positive thinking. Their experiences demonstrate the profound impact that a positive mindset can have on personal growth, relationships, career success, and overall happiness.

So, let us embark on this incredible journey of self-discovery and personal transformation together. By embracing positive thinking, you have the opportunity to create a life filled with joy, resilience, and success. Get ready to unlock your full potential and discover the endless possibilities that await you on the path of positive thinking.

Understanding the Mind-Body Connection

In today's fast-paced world, where stress and anxiety seem to be the norm, it is essential to delve into the fascinating concept of the mind-body connection. This subchapter aims to shed light on this intricate relationship and how it can be harnessed to cultivate positive thinking and overall well-being.

The mind-body connection refers to the profound interdependence of our mental and physical states. It highlights the fact that our thoughts, emotions, and beliefs have a direct impact on our physical health and vice versa. This concept has been studied and embraced by various disciplines, including psychology, neuroscience, and alternative medicine.

Positive thinking, a powerful tool for personal growth and success, is deeply intertwined with the mind-body connection. When we adopt an optimistic mindset, our brain releases endorphins and other feel-good chemicals, which not only enhance our mood but also boost our immune system. On the other hand, negative thoughts and stress can weaken the immune system, making us more susceptible to illnesses.

Moreover, research has shown that our thoughts and emotions can influence our physical well-being on a cellular level. Studies in the field of psychoneuroimmunology have demonstrated that our mental state can impact the functioning of our immune system, affecting the body's ability to fight off diseases and heal itself.

Understanding and harnessing the mind-body connection can contribute to a more holistic approach to well-being. By cultivating positive thinking, we can create a ripple effect that permeates every aspect of our lives. Positive thoughts not only boost our physical health but also enhance our relationships, increase our resilience in the face of challenges, and improve our overall happiness.

To tap into the power of the mind-body connection, it is crucial to engage in practices that promote mindfulness, such as meditation, deep breathing exercises, and visualization. These techniques allow us to quiet our minds, focus on the present moment, and become more aware of the connection between our thoughts and bodily sensations.

In conclusion, the mind-body connection is a profound and vital aspect of our lives. By understanding and nurturing this connection, we can harness the power of positive thinking to cultivate growth and success in every aspect of our lives, from our health and relationships to our personal and professional endeavors. Embracing this concept and incorporating it into our daily lives can lead to a more fulfilling and joyful existence.

Benefits of Positive Thinking

Positive thinking is a powerful tool that can transform your life and bring about numerous benefits. In this subchapter, we will explore the various advantages that positive thinking can have on your overall well-being and success. Whether you are a student, professional, parent, or anyone seeking personal growth, the benefits of positive thinking are applicable to all.

1. Improved Mental Health: Positive thinking has a profound impact on your mental well-being. It helps reduce stress, anxiety, and depression by promoting a more optimistic and hopeful mindset. By focusing on the positive aspects of life, you can overcome negative thoughts and develop resilience in the face of challenges.

2. Increased Confidence and Self-Esteem: Positive thinking allows you to recognize your strengths and capabilities. By cultivating a positive mindset, you develop a sense of belief in yourself, leading to increased self-confidence and higher self-esteem. This newfound confidence empowers you to take on new opportunities and achieve your goals.

3. Enhanced Physical Health: Research has shown that positive thinking has a positive correlation with improved physical health. When you maintain a positive outlook, your stress levels decrease, leading to lower blood pressure, improved immune function, and a reduced risk of chronic diseases. Positive thinkers also tend to engage in healthier lifestyle habits such as regular exercise and a balanced diet.

4. Better Relationships: Positive thinking not only benefits your own well-being but also positively impacts your relationships with others. By radiating positivity, you attract like-minded individuals and build

stronger connections. Your positive attitude can inspire and uplift those around you, fostering healthier and more fulfilling relationships.

5. Increased Productivity and Success: Positive thinking helps you develop a growth mindset, enabling you to see failures as opportunities for growth. With a positive outlook, you become more motivated, focused, and resilient in pursuing your goals. This, in turn, leads to increased productivity and a higher likelihood of achieving success in various aspects of life.

6. Improved Problem-Solving Skills: By approaching challenges with a positive mindset, you are able to think creatively and find solutions more effectively. Positive thinking broadens your perspective, allowing you to see possibilities and alternatives that may have otherwise been overlooked. This enhances your problem-solving skills and enables you to overcome obstacles more efficiently.

In conclusion, positive thinking has numerous benefits that can positively impact every aspect of your life. By cultivating a positive mindset, you can improve your mental and physical health, boost your confidence, build stronger relationships, increase productivity, and enhance problem-solving abilities. Embracing the power of positive thinking is a transformative step toward nurturing growth and achieving success in all areas of life.

Overcoming Negative Thought Patterns

In our journey towards personal growth and success, one of the biggest hurdles we often face is the presence of negative thought patterns. These patterns can hinder our progress, drain our energy, and limit our potential. However, with the right mindset and tools, we can overcome these patterns and cultivate a more positive and empowered outlook on life.

Negative thought patterns can manifest in various ways, such as self-doubt, pessimism, fear of failure, or constant comparison to others. These patterns are often deeply ingrained within us, having been shaped by past experiences, upbringing, or societal influences. But it is important to remember that we have the power to break free from them and create a more positive mindset.

The first step in overcoming negative thought patterns is self-awareness. We must recognize and acknowledge the presence of these patterns in our lives. Take a moment to reflect on your thoughts and emotions. Are there recurring negative patterns that hold you back from reaching your full potential? Identifying these patterns is essential for initiating change.

Once we have become aware of our negative thought patterns, it is crucial to challenge and reframe them. Instead of dwelling on self-doubt or fear, we can choose to focus on our strengths, accomplishments, and potential for growth. Practice positive affirmations and visualize yourself successfully overcoming challenges. By consciously replacing negative thoughts with positive ones, we can gradually rewire our brains to adopt a more optimistic outlook.

Another effective strategy is surrounding ourselves with positive influences. Seek out individuals who radiate positivity and inspire you to be your best self. Engage in activities that uplift your spirit and bring you joy. By immersing ourselves in positive environments, we can create a supportive network that encourages us to overcome negative thought patterns and embrace a more positive mindset.

Additionally, practicing gratitude can be a powerful tool in combating negative thought patterns. Take time each day to reflect on the things you are grateful for, no matter how small they may seem. Shifting our focus towards gratitude helps us appreciate the positive aspects of our lives and reduces the impact of negative thoughts.

Overcoming negative thought patterns is an ongoing process that requires patience, persistence, and self-compassion. It is important to remember that setbacks may occur, but each setback is an opportunity for growth. By consistently challenging and reframing negative thoughts, surrounding ourselves with positivity, and practicing gratitude, we can gradually transform our mindset and create a more fulfilling and successful life.

In conclusion, overcoming negative thought patterns is essential for nurturing growth and success in every aspect of life. By cultivating a positive mindset, we can unlock our true potential and embrace a more fulfilling and prosperous future. Remember, you have the power to break free from negativity and create the life you desire.

Chapter 2: Cultivating a Positive Mindset

Recognizing and Challenging Negative Self-Talk

In our journey towards personal growth and success, one of the biggest obstacles we often face is negative self-talk. It's that voice inside our heads that constantly criticizes, doubts, and belittles us. Negative self-talk can be incredibly damaging, undermining our self-confidence, motivation, and overall well-being. However, the good news is that we have the power to recognize and challenge these negative thoughts, paving the way for a more positive and fulfilling life.

The first step in combating negative self-talk is to become aware of it. Pay attention to the thoughts that arise when you encounter challenges or setbacks. Are they supportive and encouraging, or do they immediately jump to self-blame and self-doubt? Recognizing these negative narratives is crucial because only then can we begin to challenge them.

Once you've identified negative self-talk patterns, it's time to challenge them with positive affirmations and realistic perspectives. Replace self-defeating thoughts with empowering statements. For example, instead of thinking, "I'm not good enough," shift your mindset to, "I am capable and will learn and grow from this experience." By consciously replacing negative thoughts with positive ones, you can rewire your brain to focus on possibilities and solutions rather than limitations.

Another effective strategy is to seek evidence that contradicts your negative self-talk. Often, our negative thoughts stem from distorted perceptions and assumptions. Actively look for examples that prove your self-talk wrong. For instance, if you believe you always fail at a particular task, remind yourself of the times when you succeeded or made progress. This exercise helps to challenge the validity of negative self-talk and provides a more balanced perspective.

Additionally, surrounding yourself with positive influences is vital in cultivating a mindset of optimism and self-belief. Seek out supportive friends, mentors, or join communities that promote positive thinking. Engaging with like-minded individuals who share similar goals and aspirations can provide encouragement, accountability, and a fresh perspective, helping you challenge negative self-talk more effectively.

Remember, recognizing and challenging negative self-talk is an ongoing process. It requires patience, self-compassion, and consistent effort. By actively working on transforming your inner dialogue, you can build a foundation of positivity and resilience that will enhance every aspect of your life.

In "The Positivity Project: Nurturing Growth and Success in Every Aspect of Life," we delve deeper into the tools and techniques for recognizing and challenging negative self-talk. By mastering this skill, you will unlock your full potential and create a life filled with joy, fulfillment, and success. Whether you are a student, professional, or simply someone seeking personal growth, this subchapter will guide you on a transformative journey towards positive thinking and a brighter future.

Practicing Gratitude and Appreciation

In our fast-paced and often stressful lives, it can be easy to overlook the simple joys and blessings that surround us. We get caught up in our daily routines, chasing after success and constantly striving for more. However, taking a moment to cultivate gratitude and appreciation can bring about profound changes in our mindset and overall well-being. This subchapter explores the power of practicing gratitude and appreciation, and how it can nurture growth and success in every aspect of life.

Gratitude is the practice of acknowledging and appreciating the good things in our lives. It is about shifting our focus from what we lack to what we have. When we actively practice gratitude, we train our minds to seek out the positive aspects of our experiences and become more aware of the abundance around us.

Research has shown that regularly practicing gratitude can have a significant impact on our mental and emotional well-being. It has been linked to increased happiness, reduced stress levels, improved relationships, and even better physical health. By cultivating gratitude, we can rewire our brains to default to a positive outlook, fostering a more optimistic and resilient mindset.

Appreciation goes hand in hand with gratitude. It involves recognizing and valuing the efforts and contributions of others. When we express appreciation to those around us, we not only make them feel valued and supported, but we also enhance our own sense of connection and fulfillment. Appreciation fosters positive relationships, boosts morale, and creates a more harmonious environment.

Practicing gratitude and appreciation requires conscious effort and intentionality. It starts with simply taking a moment each day to reflect on the things we are grateful for. This can be as small as a beautiful sunset or as significant as the love and support of our loved ones. The key is to focus on the positive aspects and genuinely appreciate them.

Integrating gratitude practices into our daily routines can also be beneficial. This could involve keeping a gratitude journal, where we write down three things we are grateful for each day. It could also mean expressing appreciation to someone in person or through a heartfelt note. Engaging in acts of kindness and generosity is another powerful way to cultivate gratitude and appreciation.

By embracing gratitude and appreciation as a way of life, we can transform our mindset and experience a greater sense of fulfillment and joy. It allows us to recognize the abundance that already exists and opens the door to even more positivity and success. So, let us embark on this journey of practicing gratitude and appreciation, and witness the transformative effects it can have on every aspect of our lives.

Embracing Optimism and Hope

In the journey of life, we often encounter obstacles, setbacks, and challenges that can leave us feeling discouraged and defeated. However, it is during these difficult times that the power of optimism and hope becomes truly invaluable. In this subchapter, we will explore the significance of embracing optimism and hope in every aspect of life, and how it can lead to personal growth and success.

Optimism is a mindset that focuses on seeing the positive aspects of any situation. It is about looking beyond the immediate setbacks and believing that there is always a silver lining. When we choose to embrace optimism, we invite positive energy into our lives. It allows us to approach challenges with a sense of possibility and resilience, enabling us to find creative solutions and learn valuable lessons along the way. By cultivating a positive outlook, we can transform adversity into stepping stones towards personal growth and success.

Hope, on the other hand, is the unwavering belief that things will get better. It is the fuel that keeps us moving forward, even when faced with seemingly insurmountable odds. Hope gives us the strength to persevere, to keep striving for our goals, and to never give up on our dreams. It is a powerful force that can inspire and motivate us to overcome obstacles and reach new heights. When we embrace hope, we open ourselves up to endless possibilities and allow ourselves to dream big.

For those who have chosen the path of positive thinking, embracing optimism and hope becomes second nature. They understand that mindset is everything, and that their thoughts and beliefs shape their reality. By consciously choosing to focus on the positive, they attract more positivity into their lives. They understand that setbacks are temporary, and that every challenge is an opportunity for growth and self-improvement.

Embracing optimism and hope is not about denying the existence of pain or difficulties. It is about acknowledging them, but not allowing them to define us. It is about finding strength in the face of adversity and having faith that things will get better. By cultivating these qualities, we can navigate through life's ups and downs with resilience and grace.

So, dear reader, regardless of where you are in life or what challenges you may be facing, remember to embrace optimism and hope. Choose to see the glass as half full, and believe in the power of your dreams. By doing so, you will unlock a world of endless possibilities and pave the way for personal growth and success in every aspect of your life.

Developing Resilience in the Face of Challenges

Resilience is an invaluable trait that allows individuals to navigate through life's challenges with an unwavering spirit and a positive mindset. In the face of adversity, it is resilience that enables us to bounce back, learn from our experiences, and continue moving forward towards success. This subchapter of "The Positivity Project: Nurturing Growth and Success in Every Aspect of Life" aims to help individuals from all walks of life develop their resilience and harness its power to overcome obstacles.

Resilience is not an innate quality; it is a skill that can be cultivated and honed over time. By adopting certain strategies and mindsets, we can strengthen our resilience and become better equipped to handle life's ups and downs.

One of the most important factors in developing resilience is maintaining a positive outlook. Positive thinking allows us to reframe challenges as opportunities for growth and learning. Instead of dwelling on the negative aspects of a situation, we can focus on finding solutions and moving forward. By shifting our perspective, we can transform setbacks into stepping stones towards success.

Another crucial aspect of resilience is building a support system. Surrounding ourselves with positive and supportive individuals can provide us with the emotional support and encouragement we need during challenging times. Having someone to lean on and share our experiences with can make a world of difference in our ability to bounce back.

Furthermore, it is important to develop effective coping mechanisms to deal with stress and adversity. Engaging in activities that bring us joy, such as hobbies, exercise, or meditation, can help alleviate stress and recharge our mental and emotional batteries. By taking care of our well-being, we can build the resilience necessary to face challenges head-on.

Lastly, embracing failure as a stepping stone to success is a vital aspect of resilience. Failure is not the end; it is an opportunity to learn and grow. By reframing failure as a valuable lesson, we can cultivate resilience and persevere in the face of setbacks.

In conclusion, developing resilience is a crucial skill for every individual, regardless of their background or niche. By maintaining a positive outlook, building a support system, developing coping mechanisms, and embracing failure as an opportunity for growth, we can cultivate resilience and overcome life's challenges with grace and determination. This subchapter of "The Positivity Project: Nurturing Growth and Success in Every Aspect of Life" serves as a guide for individuals seeking to harness the power of resilience and thrive in every aspect of their lives.

Chapter 3: Building Positive Relationships

The Importance of Healthy Connections

In today's fast-paced and interconnected world, it is easy to get caught up in the hustle and bustle of daily life, often neglecting the importance of healthy connections. However, nurturing and maintaining positive relationships is an essential aspect of leading a fulfilling and successful life. Whether it is with family, friends, colleagues, or even acquaintances, the quality of our connections profoundly impacts our overall well-being and happiness.

Positive thinking plays a crucial role in establishing and nurturing healthy connections. When we approach relationships with a positive mindset, it allows us to foster deeper connections, empathy, and understanding. By focusing on the strengths and virtues of others, we create an environment that encourages growth and positivity. This, in turn, leads to stronger bonds, increased trust, and a greater sense of belonging.

Furthermore, healthy connections have a significant impact on our mental and emotional health. Numerous studies have shown that individuals with strong social connections experience lower levels of stress, anxiety, and depression. When we surround ourselves with positive and uplifting people, we are more likely to feel supported, understood, and encouraged. These connections provide a valuable support system during challenging times and can help us navigate through life's ups and downs with greater resilience.

Additionally, healthy connections contribute to personal and professional success. Positive relationships can open doors to new opportunities, collaborations, and mentorships. They provide a network of individuals who can offer guidance, advice, and support in various aspects of life. By surrounding ourselves with like-minded individuals who share our values and goals, we can tap into their knowledge and experience, enabling us to grow and succeed in every aspect of our lives.

It is important to note that healthy connections are not limited to personal relationships alone. Building positive connections in the workplace is equally vital. Positive thinking fosters a collaborative and supportive work environment, where employees feel valued and motivated. When individuals feel connected to their colleagues, it enhances teamwork, productivity, and overall job satisfaction.

In conclusion, the importance of healthy connections cannot be overstated. Positive thinking is the foundation upon which these connections are built. By cultivating an optimistic mindset, we create an environment that nurtures growth, fosters resilience, and enhances our overall well-being. So, let us prioritize building and maintaining healthy connections, as they are the key to leading a fulfilling and successful life in every aspect.

Enhancing Communication and Active Listening Skills

Communication is the foundation of human interaction. It plays a vital role in fostering positive relationships, resolving conflicts, and achieving personal and professional success. In today's fast-paced world, where distractions are abundant, enhancing communication and active listening skills has become more important than ever.

The ability to effectively communicate and actively listen is not only valuable in personal relationships but also in the workplace. It can greatly impact your career growth and success. By honing these skills, you can improve your relationships with colleagues, superiors, and clients, leading to a more positive and harmonious work environment.

Active listening is a crucial aspect of communication that is often overlooked. It involves fully focusing on and understanding the speaker's message without interrupting or passing judgment. By actively listening, you demonstrate respect and empathy towards the speaker, which in turn strengthens the connection and trust between both parties.

To enhance your active listening skills, start by eliminating distractions. Put away your phone, close your laptop, and give your undivided attention to the speaker. Maintain eye contact and use non-verbal cues such as nodding or smiling to show your engagement. Practice empathy by putting yourself in the speaker's shoes and trying to understand their perspective.

Effective communication goes hand in hand with active listening. It involves clearly expressing your thoughts, ideas, and emotions in a way that is easily understood by others. To enhance your communication skills, consider the following tips:

1. Be mindful of your body language and tone of voice, as they can greatly impact the message you convey.
2. Use clear and concise language, avoiding jargon or complicated terms that may confuse the listener.
3. Practice active and assertive communication by actively seeking feedback, asking clarifying questions, and expressing your thoughts and needs confidently.
4. Be open-minded and receptive to feedback, as it provides an opportunity for growth and improvement.

By enhancing your communication and active listening skills, you can foster a more positive and supportive environment in every aspect of your life. Whether it's in personal relationships, the workplace, or even in your own self-talk, positive thinking is essential for overall well-being and success.

Remember, effective communication is a continuous learning process. It requires practice, patience, and a commitment to self-improvement. Embrace the journey of enhancing your communication and active listening skills, and you will reap the rewards of stronger relationships, increased productivity, and a more positive outlook on life.

Nurturing Empathy and Compassion

Empathy and compassion are powerful emotions that have the ability to transform our lives and the lives of those around us. They have the potential to create a ripple effect of positivity, fostering growth and success in every aspect of life. In this subchapter, we will explore the importance of nurturing empathy and compassion and how it can enhance our journey towards positive thinking.

Empathy is the ability to understand and share the feelings of others. It allows us to put ourselves in someone else's shoes, to truly see the world from their perspective. When we practice empathy, we are able to connect with others on a deeper level, building stronger relationships and fostering a sense of belonging.

Compassion, on the other hand, is the desire to alleviate the suffering of others. It is an active expression of empathy, a willingness to take action and make a positive difference in someone's life. When we practice compassion, we become agents of change, spreading kindness and love wherever we go.

Nurturing empathy and compassion starts with self-awareness. We must first understand and acknowledge our own emotions before we can truly empathize with others. Taking the time to reflect on our own experiences and emotions allows us to develop a sense of empathy that is genuine and heartfelt.

Once we have cultivated empathy within ourselves, we can then extend it towards others. This involves active listening, seeking to understand without judgment, and offering support and validation. By showing empathy towards others, we create a safe space for them to be vulnerable and share their experiences.

Compassion, on the other hand, requires action. It involves actively looking for ways to help others, whether through acts of kindness, volunteering, or simply lending a listening ear. By practicing compassion, we not only make a positive impact on those around us, but we also experience a sense of fulfillment and purpose in our own lives.

Nurturing empathy and compassion is not always easy, especially in a world that can be chaotic and fast-paced. However, by incorporating small acts of empathy and compassion into our daily lives, we can create a ripple effect of positivity that not only enhances our own well-being but also spreads to those around us.

In conclusion, nurturing empathy and compassion is an essential aspect of positive thinking. By developing these qualities within ourselves, we create a foundation for personal growth and success. Let us strive to be more empathetic and compassionate towards ourselves and others, and together, we can create a world filled with understanding, kindness, and love.

Resolving Conflict Positively

In life, conflicts are inevitable. Whether they arise in our personal relationships, workplace, or even within ourselves, conflicts can often leave us feeling stressed, frustrated, and drained. However, it is important to remember that conflict, when approached with a positive mindset, can lead to personal growth, improved relationships, and increased success in every aspect of life.

Resolving conflict positively is a skill that can be learned and cultivated by anyone, regardless of their background or experiences. By adopting a positive thinking mindset during conflicts, we can transform these challenging situations into opportunities for growth and understanding.

One of the first steps in resolving conflict positively is to approach it with an open mind and empathy. This means actively listening to the other person's perspective without judgment and trying to understand their point of view. By doing so, we create an environment of mutual respect and trust, allowing for a more productive and collaborative resolution.

Another essential element in resolving conflict positively is effective communication. It is important to express our thoughts and feelings in a clear and respectful manner, using "I" statements to avoid blaming or accusing others. By focusing on our own experiences and emotions, we can foster a more constructive dialogue and encourage the other person to do the same.

Furthermore, finding common ground and seeking win-win solutions can be instrumental in resolving conflicts positively. Instead of approaching conflicts as a competition where one person must win and the other must lose, we can strive for solutions that benefit both parties. This approach promotes collaboration and cooperation, leading to long-lasting resolutions and strengthened relationships.

In addition to these strategies, self-awareness and self-reflection play a crucial role in resolving conflict positively. Taking the time to understand our own triggers and reactions can help us respond more effectively to conflict situations. By recognizing our own biases and limitations, we can approach conflicts with humility and a willingness to learn and grow from the experience.

Ultimately, resolving conflict positively requires practice and a commitment to personal growth. By embracing a positive thinking mindset and implementing these strategies, we can transform conflicts into opportunities for growth and success in every aspect of our lives. Remember, conflicts are not obstacles; they are stepping stones toward a more fulfilling and harmonious existence.

Chapter 4: Achieving Personal Growth and Success

Setting Goals and Visualizing Success

In the pursuit of personal growth and success, one of the most powerful tools at our disposal is the ability to set goals and visualize our desired outcomes. This subchapter will delve into the importance of setting goals and harnessing the power of positive thinking to manifest success in every aspect of life.

Goals serve as guideposts, providing us with a clear direction and purpose. Without goals, we may find ourselves wandering aimlessly, lacking motivation and a sense of fulfillment. By setting specific, measurable, attainable, relevant, and time-bound (SMART) goals, we create a roadmap that leads us towards our aspirations.

Positive thinking is the driving force behind goal achievement. When we approach our goals with a positive mindset, we cultivate a belief in our abilities and attract the necessary resources and opportunities. Positive thinking allows us to overcome obstacles and setbacks, enabling us to stay focused and determined on our path towards success.

Visualizing success is a powerful technique that reinforces positive thinking and propels us towards our goals. By vividly imagining ourselves accomplishing our goals, we create a mental blueprint for success. This visualization technique activates the subconscious mind, aligning our thoughts, emotions, and actions with our desired outcomes. As we consistently visualize success, we begin to attract the circumstances and opportunities that will help us achieve our goals.

In order to effectively set goals and visualize success, it is essential to adopt a growth mindset. Embracing a growth mindset means viewing setbacks and challenges as opportunities for learning and growth. With a growth mindset, we understand that our abilities and intelligence can be developed through effort and persistence. This mindset fuels our motivation, resilience, and willingness to take risks, ultimately paving the way for success.

Throughout this subchapter, we will explore various strategies and techniques for setting goals and visualizing success. From creating a vision board to practicing affirmations and utilizing visualization exercises, we will provide practical tools for harnessing the power of positive thinking and turning our goals into reality.

By setting goals and visualizing success, we empower ourselves to create the life we desire. This subchapter aims to inspire and guide every individual, regardless of their background or circumstances, to embrace positive thinking and unlock their full potential. With the right mindset and tools, success becomes not just a distant dream, but an achievable reality.

Harnessing the Power of Self-Discipline and Motivation

In our journey towards personal growth and success, two key elements play a vital role: self-discipline and motivation. These powerful forces have the potential to transform our lives and propel us towards achieving our goals and dreams. In this subchapter, we will explore the significance of self-discipline and motivation and learn how to harness their power to lead a more fulfilling and successful life.

Self-discipline is the cornerstone of personal development. It is the ability to control our impulses, stay focused, and take consistent action towards our goals. Without self-discipline, our dreams remain distant fantasies, and our potential goes untapped. However, by cultivating self-discipline, we can overcome obstacles, develop positive habits, and achieve extraordinary results.

One way to enhance self-discipline is by setting clear and specific goals. When we have a clear vision of what we want to achieve, it becomes easier to stay disciplined and motivated. Breaking our goals into smaller, manageable tasks and creating a timeline helps us stay on track and maintain our focus.

Motivation, on the other hand, is the driving force behind our actions. It is the spark that ignites our passion and propels us forward, even in the face of challenges. Cultivating a positive mindset and surrounding ourselves with inspiration and positivity can boost our motivation levels significantly.

To harness the power of motivation, it is crucial to understand our intrinsic and extrinsic motivations. Intrinsic motivation comes from within and is fueled by our personal desires, values, and passions.

Extrinsic motivation, on the other hand, stems from external rewards or recognition. By aligning our goals with our intrinsic motivations, we can tap into a limitless source of inspiration and drive.

Developing self-discipline and motivation requires consistent practice and perseverance. It is essential to recognize that setbacks and failures are part of the journey. Instead of succumbing to self-doubt or negativity, we must embrace these challenges as opportunities for growth and learning. By staying resilient and committed, we can overcome any obstacles that come our way.

In conclusion, self-discipline and motivation are the building blocks of personal growth and success. By harnessing their power, we can transform our lives and achieve our dreams. Cultivating self-discipline through goal-setting and breaking tasks into manageable steps enables us to stay focused and take consistent action. Meanwhile, understanding intrinsic and extrinsic motivations helps us tap into a limitless well of inspiration. With perseverance and a positive mindset, we can embrace challenges and turn them into stepping stones towards our desired outcomes. So, let us embark on this journey of self-discovery, armed with the power of self-discipline and motivation, and unlock our true potential for success and happiness in every aspect of life.

Embracing Failure as a Stepping Stone to Success

Failure is often seen as something negative, a setback that hinders progress and success. However, in reality, failure can be a powerful catalyst for growth and development. By shifting our perspective and embracing failure as a stepping stone to success, we can unlock our true potential and achieve greatness in every aspect of life.

One of the key aspects of positive thinking is the ability to reframe challenges and setbacks as opportunities for growth. When we view failure as a valuable learning experience, we open ourselves up to new possibilities and insights. Instead of dwelling on our mistakes, we can focus on the lessons learned and use them to propel us forward.

Failure teaches us resilience and perseverance. It is through failure that we discover our strengths and weaknesses, enabling us to make necessary adjustments and improvements. Each failure brings us one step closer to success, as we gain valuable knowledge and experience along the way.

Moreover, failure provides us with an opportunity to step out of our comfort zones and take risks. By embracing failure, we become more comfortable with uncertainty and change. We learn to trust ourselves and our abilities, even in the face of adversity. This mindset shift allows us to tap into our full potential and accomplish things we never thought possible.

In addition, failure fosters innovation and creativity. When our initial plans or strategies fail, we are forced to think outside the box and come up with new approaches. This can lead to groundbreaking discoveries and solutions that we may have never considered otherwise. Failure, therefore, becomes a necessary part of the creative process, igniting our imagination and pushing us to think differently.

To embrace failure as a stepping stone to success, we must cultivate a growth mindset. This means celebrating effort, perseverance, and learning, rather than solely focusing on outcomes. By reframing failure as an opportunity for growth, we create a positive feedback loop that fuels our motivation and drive.

In conclusion, failure is not the end of the road, but rather a stepping stone to success. By embracing failure and viewing it as a valuable learning experience, we can unlock our potential, foster resilience, and drive innovation. So, let us embrace failure with open arms, for it is through our failures that we truly find success in every aspect of life.

Cultivating a Growth Mindset for Continuous Improvement

In today's fast-paced and ever-changing world, it has become increasingly important to develop a growth mindset to navigate the challenges and uncertainties that life throws at us. A growth mindset is the belief that our abilities and intelligence can be developed through dedication and hard work, rather than being fixed traits that cannot be changed. This mindset is essential for positive thinking and is the key to nurturing growth and success in every aspect of life.

One of the first steps in cultivating a growth mindset is to embrace the power of yet. When faced with a setback or failure, instead of saying "I can't do this," we should adopt the perspective of "I can't do this yet." This simple shift in mindset acknowledges that with time, effort, and perseverance, we can improve and grow. It allows us to view challenges as opportunities for learning and development, rather than insurmountable obstacles.

Another important aspect of cultivating a growth mindset is to embrace failure as a stepping stone to success. Instead of viewing failure as a reflection of our abilities, we should see it as an opportunity to learn and grow. By reframing failure in this way, we can overcome setbacks with resilience and determination. We can use failure as a springboard for continuous improvement, constantly striving to better ourselves and our circumstances.

Additionally, it is crucial to surround ourselves with positive influences and like-minded individuals who share our commitment to growth and improvement. By seeking out supportive communities and mentors, we can learn from their experiences and gain valuable insights. These connections can provide us with encouragement, accountability, and guidance on our journey toward personal and professional development.

Lastly, developing a growth mindset requires us to prioritize self-reflection and self-awareness. By regularly assessing our strengths, weaknesses, and areas for improvement, we can identify opportunities to grow and develop. This introspection allows us to set realistic goals, design action plans, and track our progress along the way.

In conclusion, cultivating a growth mindset is a powerful tool for continuous improvement and success. By embracing the power of yet, reframing failure, seeking supportive communities, and prioritizing self-reflection, we can foster positive thinking and unlock our full potential in every aspect of life. With a growth mindset, we can overcome challenges, embrace opportunities for growth, and ultimately lead a more fulfilling and successful life.

Chapter 5: Fostering Positive Habits and Routines

Establishing a Morning Routine for a Productive Day

In our fast-paced world, it's easy to get caught up in the chaos and lose sight of our goals and aspirations. However, by implementing a morning routine centered around positivity and productivity, we can set ourselves up for success in every aspect of life. Whether you're a student, a working professional, or a stay-at-home parent, a well-structured morning routine can help you start your day on the right foot and maintain a positive mindset throughout.

The key to establishing an effective morning routine is to prioritize self-care and positivity. Begin by setting your alarm clock for a consistent time each morning, allowing yourself ample time to wake up without rushing. This will provide a sense of calm and eliminate the stress of starting your day in a hurry. As you wake up, take a moment to express gratitude for the day ahead and visualize your goals, fostering a positive mindset from the get-go.

After getting out of bed, engage in activities that promote physical and mental well-being. Incorporate exercise into your routine, whether it's a short yoga session, a brisk walk, or a quick workout. Physical activity releases endorphins, boosting your mood and energy levels for the day ahead. Additionally, allocate time for mindfulness or meditation to clear your mind and enhance focus. These practices will help you approach the day with a centered and positive mindset.

To further cultivate positivity, incorporate activities that bring you joy and inspiration. This could involve reading a few pages from a motivational book, listening to uplifting podcasts, or journaling your thoughts and goals. Engaging in activities that align with your passions will ignite your creativity and motivation, setting the tone for a productive day.

Lastly, don't forget to nourish your body with a healthy breakfast and hydrate yourself. A nutritious meal will provide the energy you need to tackle the day's challenges, while staying hydrated will ensure mental clarity and overall well-being.

Remember, establishing a morning routine takes time and commitment. Start small and gradually incorporate new habits into your routine. Experiment with different activities and find what works best for you. By prioritizing self-care and positivity in the morning, you'll set the foundation for a productive and successful day, fostering growth and success in every aspect of your life.

So, embrace the power of a well-structured morning routine, and witness the transformative impact it can have on your mindset, productivity, and overall well-being. Start your day on a positive note, and let the positivity ripple through every aspect of your life.

Incorporating Mindfulness and Meditation Practices

In today's fast-paced and ever-demanding world, finding inner peace and cultivating positive thinking can seem like an impossible task. However, with the right tools and practices, anyone can achieve a state of mindfulness and incorporate meditation into their daily lives. This subchapter aims to guide you towards incorporating mindfulness and meditation practices into your routine, helping you nurture growth and success in every aspect of your life.

Mindfulness is the art of being fully present in the moment, without judgment or attachment. By practicing mindfulness, you can develop a heightened awareness of your thoughts, emotions, and surroundings. This increased self-awareness allows you to make conscious decisions and respond to situations rather than reacting impulsively. Mindfulness also helps reduce stress, anxiety, and negative thinking patterns, paving the way for a more positive and fulfilling life.

Meditation, on the other hand, is a technique that involves focusing your attention and eliminating the stream of thoughts that usually occupy your mind. Regular meditation practice can help calm your mind, improve your concentration, and promote a sense of inner peace. By setting aside dedicated time for meditation each day, even just a few minutes, you can reap the numerous benefits it offers.

To incorporate mindfulness and meditation practices into your life, start by allocating a specific time and space for these activities. Choose a quiet and comfortable spot where you won't be disturbed. Begin with short meditation sessions, gradually increasing the duration as you become more comfortable. There are various meditation techniques to explore, such as deep breathing exercises, guided visualizations, or mantra repetition. Find the method that resonates with you the most and experiment with different approaches.

Additionally, integrating mindfulness into your daily activities can be immensely beneficial. Practice mindful eating by savoring each bite, paying attention to the flavors and textures of your food. Engage in mindful walking by focusing on the sensations in your feet and the rhythm of your steps. Incorporate mindful listening by giving your full attention to conversations, truly hearing and understanding the words of others.

Remember, incorporating mindfulness and meditation practices into your life is a journey, and consistency is key. Be patient with yourself and embrace the process. Over time, you will notice the positive impact these practices have on your overall well-being, fostering personal growth, and enhancing your ability to succeed in every aspect of your life.

So why wait? Take a deep breath, close your eyes, and embark on a transformative journey towards a more positive and fulfilled life through mindfulness and meditation practices.

Prioritizing Self-Care and Wellbeing

In a world that often glorifies busyness and achievement, it is crucial to recognize the importance of prioritizing self-care and wellbeing. In this subchapter, we will delve into the significance of taking care of ourselves and cultivating a positive mindset, as well as provide practical tips to help you incorporate self-care into your daily life.

Self-care is not a luxury; it is a necessity. It is about intentionally taking care of your physical, mental, and emotional health. When we neglect ourselves, we risk burnout, decreased productivity, and a diminished sense of overall happiness. Prioritizing self-care means acknowledging that your well-being is just as important as any other aspect of your life.

One of the first steps towards prioritizing self-care is adopting a positive mindset. Positive thinking is a powerful tool that can transform your life. It involves focusing on the good, practicing gratitude, and reframing negative thoughts into positive ones. By cultivating a positive mindset, you can increase your resilience, boost your self-confidence, and improve your overall well-being.

To incorporate self-care into your daily routine, it is essential to create healthy habits. This can include activities such as exercise, meditation, journaling, or spending time in nature. These activities help reduce stress, improve sleep, and enhance overall physical and mental health. Remember to schedule time for yourself and treat it as a non-negotiable appointment. By making self-care a priority, you are investing in yourself and setting the foundation for a happier and more fulfilling life.

Additionally, it is important to set boundaries and learn to say no. By understanding your limits and not overextending yourself, you can avoid burnout and preserve your energy for the things that truly matter. Remember, saying no is not selfish; it is an act of self-care.

Lastly, surround yourself with positivity. Surrounding yourself with positive people, engaging in uplifting activities, and consuming positive media can significantly impact your mindset. Positive thinking is contagious, and by surrounding yourself with it, you are more likely to maintain a positive outlook on life.

In conclusion, prioritizing self-care and wellbeing is crucial for everyone, especially those seeking to cultivate a positive mindset. By taking care of ourselves, we not only enhance our own well-being but also become better equipped to navigate life's challenges and nurture growth and success in every aspect. So, take a moment to assess your self-care needs and commit to making yourself a priority. Your mind, body, and spirit will thank you, and you will be better equipped to spread positivity in every area of your life.

Creating a Positive Environment for Success

In order to achieve success in every aspect of life, it is crucial to cultivate a positive environment. A positive mindset plays a significant role in shaping our thoughts, actions, and outcomes. When we embrace positive thinking, we unlock our true potential and open doors to new opportunities. This subchapter explores the importance of creating a positive environment for success and provides practical tips to foster positivity in our lives.

Our environment greatly influences our thoughts and emotions. Surrounding ourselves with positivity can have a profound impact on our overall well-being and success. It is essential to eliminate negative influences and replace them with positive ones. This can include spending time with supportive and like-minded individuals who encourage personal growth and uplift our spirits. Additionally, engaging in activities that bring joy and fulfillment, such as hobbies or volunteering, can create a positive atmosphere.

A positive environment is built on the foundation of positive thinking. It involves developing an optimistic outlook towards life, challenges, and setbacks. Positive thinking enables us to focus on solutions rather than dwelling on problems. It empowers us to embrace change, take risks, and learn from failures. When we maintain a positive mindset, we attract positive experiences and people into our lives, which ultimately leads to success.

To create a positive environment, it is important to practice self-care. Taking care of our physical, mental, and emotional well-being is crucial for maintaining a positive mindset. This can involve adopting healthy habits like regular exercise, proper nutrition, and quality sleep. Engaging in mindfulness activities, such as meditation or journaling, can also help to cultivate a positive mindset and reduce stress.

Another key aspect of creating a positive environment is practicing gratitude. Expressing gratitude for the blessings in our lives, both big and small, fosters a sense of appreciation and contentment. It shifts our focus from what we lack to what we have, promoting a positive outlook. By incorporating gratitude practices into our daily routine, such as keeping a gratitude journal or expressing gratitude to others, we can create an environment that nurtures positivity and success.

In conclusion, creating a positive environment is essential for nurturing growth and success in every aspect of life. By surrounding ourselves with positivity, adopting a positive mindset, practicing self-care, and expressing gratitude, we can create an environment that fosters personal and professional achievements. Embracing positivity and incorporating these practices into our lives will empower us to overcome challenges, seize opportunities, and live a fulfilling and successful life.

Chapter 6: Spreading Positivity in the World

The Ripple Effect of Positive Actions

In a world that often seems overwhelmed by negativity and despair, it is crucial to recognize the power of positive actions and their ability to create a ripple effect that can transform lives and communities. Each one of us has the capacity to make a difference and contribute to a brighter, more uplifting world. This subchapter delves into the profound impact of positive actions and the ripple effect they can have on our lives and the lives of those around us.

Positive thinking is the foundation upon which these actions are built. It is the mindset that allows us to see opportunities in challenges, find silver linings in difficult situations, and believe in the inherent goodness within ourselves and others. When we approach life with positivity, we radiate energy that is infectious, inspiring those around us to adopt a similar outlook.

The ripple effect of positive actions begins with small gestures of kindness and compassion. A smile to a stranger, a helping hand to someone in need, or a supportive word to a friend can set off a chain reaction of positivity. These acts have the power to brighten someone's day, restore their faith in humanity, and motivate them to pay it forward.

Furthermore, positive actions have a transformative effect on our own lives. When we engage in acts of kindness and generosity, we experience a sense of fulfillment and purpose. These actions reinforce our belief in our own capabilities and remind us of the inherent goodness within us. As we witness the positive impact of our actions, we are encouraged to continue spreading positivity, creating a cycle of growth and success in every aspect of our lives.

The ripple effect extends beyond individuals and into communities. When positive actions are multiplied, they create a collective force that can bring about significant change. Imagine a community where everyone is committed to acts of kindness, empathy, and support. The synergy of these actions can lead to the creation of a thriving, harmonious society where everyone feels valued and uplifted.

In conclusion, the ripple effect of positive actions is a powerful force that has the potential to transform lives, communities, and even the world. By cultivating a positive mindset and engaging in small acts of kindness, we can create a ripple effect that spreads far and wide. Let us remember that our actions matter, and each positive action we take contributes to a brighter, more compassionate world for everyone. Embrace the power of positivity and let your actions be the catalyst for change.

Acts of Kindness and Generosity

In a world that sometimes feels filled with negativity and selfishness, it is essential to focus on the power of kindness and generosity. Acts of kindness not only bring joy and positivity to the receiver but also have a profound impact on the giver. This subchapter delves into the transformative effect of acts of kindness and generosity, empowering individuals to embrace a more positive and fulfilling life.

Kindness is a simple yet impactful action that has the power to change lives. It can be as small as offering a smile to a stranger or as significant as volunteering at a local homeless shelter. Regardless of its scale, every act of kindness has a ripple effect, spreading positivity and inspiring others to follow suit. By engaging in acts of kindness, we create a virtuous cycle that encourages the growth of a compassionate and supportive community.

Generosity, too, plays a vital role in fostering positive thinking and personal growth. When we give freely without expecting anything in return, we tap into a wellspring of abundance within ourselves. Generosity can take various forms, from donating money or possessions to sharing our time, skills, or knowledge with others. Each act of generosity contributes to a more harmonious society, where individuals support and uplift one another.

By practicing acts of kindness and generosity, we cultivate a mindset of abundance and gratitude. We develop an awareness of the interconnectedness of all beings, understanding that our actions have far-reaching consequences. These acts not only benefit others but also enhance our own well-being and happiness. Research has shown that engaging in acts of kindness and generosity leads to increased levels of joy, improved mental health, and a greater sense of purpose in life.

Incorporating acts of kindness and generosity into our daily lives can be as simple as making a conscious effort to be kind to ourselves and others. It may involve volunteering, donating to charitable causes, or actively seeking opportunities to help those in need. By adopting a mindset of kindness and generosity, we create a positive feedback loop, attracting more positivity and abundance into our lives.

In conclusion, acts of kindness and generosity are not only essential for the well-being of others but also for our own personal growth and happiness. By embracing these values, we contribute to the creation of a more compassionate and supportive world. Let us remember that every small act of kindness makes a difference, and together, we can create a positive and fulfilling life for ourselves and those around us.

Promoting Social Connection and Community Engagement

In our fast-paced and digitally driven world, it is easy to feel disconnected from others and the community around us. However, fostering social connections and engaging with our communities is essential for our overall well-being and success. In this subchapter, we will explore the importance of promoting social connection and community engagement, and how it can contribute to our positive thinking and personal growth.

Social connections are the threads that weave our lives together, providing us with a sense of belonging, support, and purpose. When we engage with others on a deeper level, we not only strengthen our own mental and emotional well-being but also contribute to the collective happiness of our community. By actively seeking out opportunities to connect with others, we open ourselves up to new experiences, perspectives, and friendships.

Community engagement is another vital aspect of leading a fulfilling life. When we actively participate in our communities, whether through volunteering, attending local events, or getting involved in community organizations, we contribute to the greater good. Not only does community engagement create a positive impact on those around us, but it also allows us to develop a sense of purpose and meaning in our lives.

Promoting social connection and community engagement can significantly enhance our positive thinking. By surrounding ourselves with like-minded individuals who share our values and aspirations, we create a support system that uplifts and motivates us. Through collaborative efforts and shared experiences, we can overcome challenges and achieve greater success in our personal and professional lives.

Furthermore, social connection and community engagement provide opportunities for personal growth. By stepping outside of our comfort zones and engaging with diverse groups of people, we learn about different cultures, perspectives, and ways of life. This exposure broadens our horizons, fosters empathy, and helps us become more well-rounded individuals.

To actively promote social connection and community engagement, we can take small but meaningful steps. These may include joining local clubs or organizations, attending community events, volunteering for a cause close to our hearts, or even simply striking up conversations with strangers. By making a conscious effort to connect with others and engage in our communities, we create a ripple effect that can transform not only our own lives but the entire community.

In conclusion, promoting social connection and community engagement is crucial for our overall well-being, personal growth, and success. By actively seeking out opportunities to connect with others and engage with our communities, we open ourselves up to new experiences, perspectives, and friendships. Through collaborative efforts and shared experiences, we can overcome challenges, achieve success, and foster positive thinking. So, let us embrace the power of social connection and community engagement, and create a world where everyone feels a sense of belonging and purpose.

Inspiring Others to Embrace Positivity

In a world filled with challenges and uncertainties, it is crucial to foster a positive mindset that can transform both our own lives and the lives of those around us. This subchapter aims to inspire individuals from all walks of life to embrace positivity and harness its remarkable power. Whether you are a student, a professional, a parent, or simply someone seeking personal growth, this section will equip you with the tools to cultivate a positive outlook and spread its influence to others.

Positive thinking is not just a fleeting state of mind; it is a lifestyle that can be cultivated and practiced. By choosing to focus on the bright side of situations and adopting an optimistic attitude, we can improve our overall well-being and enhance our chances of success. This subchapter will delve into the various benefits of positive thinking, including increased resilience, improved mental health, and stronger relationships.

To inspire others, we must first embody positivity in our own lives. By sharing personal stories and experiences, we can demonstrate the transformative power of positive thinking. Through the anecdotes and lessons shared in this subchapter, readers will gain valuable insights into how embracing positivity can lead to personal growth, better decision-making, and increased motivation.

Furthermore, this section will explore practical strategies and techniques for nurturing positivity in daily life. From gratitude practices and mindfulness exercises to affirmations and visualization, there are numerous tools we can utilize to cultivate a positive mindset. This subchapter will provide step-by-step guidance on how to incorporate these practices into our routines and encourage readers to embark on their own journey towards a more positive life.

Inspiring others to embrace positivity goes beyond personal growth; it also entails creating a ripple effect that spreads throughout our communities. By radiating positivity, we can uplift those around us, inspiring them to adopt a similar mindset. This subchapter will emphasize the importance of leading by example and fostering a supportive and encouraging environment that nurtures positivity in others. Whether it's through kind words, acts of generosity, or simply being a positive presence, we can inspire others to embrace a more optimistic outlook on life.

In conclusion, this subchapter of "The Positivity Project: Nurturing Growth and Success in Every Aspect of Life" aims to inspire individuals from all backgrounds to embrace positivity. By sharing personal stories, practical strategies, and emphasizing the importance of leading by example, readers will be equipped with the tools to cultivate a positive mindset and inspire others to do the same. Together, we can create a world where positivity thrives, fostering growth and success in every aspect of life.

Chapter 7: Overcoming Obstacles to Positivity

Identifying and Managing Stress

In our fast-paced and demanding world, stress has become an inevitable part of our lives. Whether it's work-related pressure, personal challenges, or even the current state of the world, stress can take a toll on our mental and physical well-being. However, by understanding and effectively managing stress, we can maintain a positive mindset and lead a fulfilling life.

The first step in managing stress is to identify its causes. Take a moment to reflect on the situations or circumstances that trigger stress for you. It could be deadlines at work, relationship issues, financial worries, or even everyday hassles. By pinpointing these stressors, you can begin to develop strategies to cope with them proactively.

Once you have identified the sources of stress, it's important to recognize the signs and symptoms of stress. These can manifest in various ways, such as irritability, anxiety, difficulty concentrating, changes in appetite or sleep patterns, and even physical ailments like headaches or muscle tension. Paying attention to these signals can help you take timely action to prevent stress from escalating.

Positive thinking plays a crucial role in managing stress. By adopting an optimistic mindset, you can change your perception of stress and view it as a challenge rather than a threat. Engage in positive self-talk and remind yourself that you have the ability to overcome any obstacles that come your way. Surround yourself with positive influences, whether it's supportive friends and family or inspiring books and media. Cultivating gratitude and focusing on the good things in your life can also shift your perspective and reduce stress levels.

Implementing effective stress management techniques is essential. Regular exercise, deep breathing exercises, and meditation can help relax your body and mind. Engaging in activities you enjoy, such as hobbies or spending time in nature, can provide an outlet for stress and promote a sense of well-being. Time management techniques, such as prioritizing tasks and setting realistic goals, can also alleviate stress by providing a sense of control and accomplishment.

Remember, managing stress is an ongoing process, and what works for one person may not work for another. It's important to experiment with different strategies and find what works best for you. By identifying and managing stress effectively, you can maintain a positive mindset, nurture personal growth, and achieve success in every aspect of your life.

Overcoming Self-Doubt and Fear

In life, we often find ourselves grappling with self-doubt and fear. These negative emotions can hold us back from reaching our full potential and experiencing true happiness. However, it is crucial to understand that self-doubt and fear are not permanent states of mind; they can be overcome with the power of positive thinking.

Self-doubt often stems from a lack of confidence in our abilities and a fear of failure. We question our worthiness and constantly compare ourselves to others, resulting in a never-ending cycle of negativity. However, it is important to realize that self-doubt is merely a perception and not an accurate reflection of our capabilities.

To overcome self-doubt, we must cultivate a mindset of positivity. This involves recognizing our strengths and celebrating our achievements, no matter how small they may seem. By focusing on our successes, we can gradually build our confidence and silence the voice of self-doubt.

Fear, on the other hand, is often born out of the unknown. We fear what we cannot control or predict, and this fear can paralyze us, preventing us from taking risks and pursuing our dreams. However, it is important to remember that fear is a natural human emotion and can be conquered.

To conquer fear, we must face it head-on. This involves stepping out of our comfort zones and taking calculated risks. By embracing uncertainty, we open ourselves up to new opportunities and experiences. It is through these challenges that we grow and learn to trust in ourselves and our abilities.

Positive thinking is a powerful tool in overcoming self-doubt and fear. By adopting a positive mindset, we can reframe our thoughts and focus on the possibilities rather than the limitations. This shift in perspective allows us to approach challenges with optimism and resilience.

In "The Positivity Project: Nurturing Growth and Success in Every Aspect of Life," we delve into the techniques and strategies that can help you overcome self-doubt and fear. Through real-life examples, inspiring stories, and practical exercises, this subchapter provides a comprehensive guide to shifting your mindset and embracing positivity.

Remember, everyone faces moments of self-doubt and fear. However, it is how we choose to respond to these emotions that determines our success and happiness. By adopting a positive mindset and cultivating self-belief, you can overcome any obstacle and achieve greatness in every aspect of life. Start your journey towards a more positive and fulfilling life today!

Dealing with Criticism and Negativity

Criticism and negativity are inevitable aspects of life that we all encounter at some point. Whether it comes from our peers, colleagues, or even ourselves, it can often be challenging to handle and can greatly impact our well-being and overall positivity. However, learning how to deal with criticism and negativity effectively is essential for personal growth and success. In this subchapter, we will explore various strategies and techniques to help you navigate through these challenging situations, fostering a mindset of positive thinking.

The first step in dealing with criticism and negativity is to develop self-awareness. Understand that criticism is not a reflection of your worth as an individual, but rather a perspective or opinion of others. By separating yourself from the criticism, you can evaluate it objectively and determine if it holds any merit. This self-awareness will allow you to filter out unjustified negativity and focus on constructive feedback that can aid your personal and professional growth.

Another powerful tool in handling criticism is to practice empathy. Try to understand the emotions and intentions behind the negative comments or actions of others. Often, people express criticism out of their own fears, insecurities, or personal frustrations. By empathizing with their perspective, you can respond in a compassionate and understanding manner, diffusing the negativity and potentially even turning it into a productive conversation.

Additionally, it is crucial to develop resilience when faced with criticism or negativity. Rather than allowing it to bring you down, use it as an opportunity for self-improvement. Embrace the mindset of continuous learning and growth, recognizing that constructive criticism can help you identify areas for improvement and propel you towards success.

Finally, surround yourself with a positive support system. Seek out individuals who believe in your abilities, encourage your growth, and provide constructive feedback. Their support can serve as a buffer against negativity, giving you the strength and confidence to overcome any criticism that comes your way.

Remember, dealing with criticism and negativity is a skill that can be mastered with time and practice. By cultivating self-awareness, empathy, resilience, and a positive support system, you can navigate through these challenges while maintaining a mindset of positive thinking. Embrace criticism as an opportunity for growth, and let negativity fuel your determination to succeed.

Maintaining Positivity in Challenging Situations

In life, we often face various challenges that can easily dampen our spirits and drain our positivity. Whether it's a setback at work, a personal crisis, or a global pandemic, maintaining a positive mindset becomes crucial to navigate through these difficult times. This subchapter aims to provide valuable insights and strategies for cultivating and preserving positivity, even in the face of adversity.

One of the fundamental principles of positive thinking is to focus on gratitude. When we shift our attention towards the things we are grateful for, we create a foundation of positivity that can withstand any challenge. Take time each day to reflect on the blessings in your life, no matter how small they may seem. It could be as simple as appreciating a beautiful sunrise, a supportive friend, or a delicious meal. By consciously cultivating gratitude, we train our minds to see the silver linings.

Another powerful tool for maintaining positivity is self-care. During challenging situations, it's essential to prioritize your mental, emotional, and physical well-being. Engage in activities that bring you joy and relaxation, such as exercise, meditation, or spending time in nature. Surround yourself with positive influences, whether it be through uplifting books, podcasts, or supportive relationships. Remember, taking care of yourself is not selfish; it's necessary to stay resilient and optimistic.

Furthermore, reframing negative thoughts is a key component of positive thinking. Instead of dwelling on the problems, focus on finding solutions and opportunities for growth. Train your mind to see challenges as stepping stones towards personal development. Each setback becomes a chance to learn, adapt, and ultimately succeed. By shifting your perspective, you can transform obstacles into opportunities for growth and maintain a positive outlook.

Lastly, fostering a sense of community and connection is vital in tough times. Surround yourself with like-minded individuals who share your commitment to positivity. Engage in acts of kindness and generosity, as giving back not only uplifts others but also boosts your own sense of purpose and fulfillment.

In conclusion, maintaining positivity in challenging situations is a lifelong practice that requires conscious effort and dedication. By cultivating gratitude, practicing self-care, reframing negative thoughts, and fostering a sense of community, you can preserve your positivity even in the most difficult times. Remember, positive thinking is not about denying reality; it's about harnessing the power of optimism to navigate adversity with grace and resilience. Embrace the power of positivity and watch as it transforms your life in every aspect.

Chapter 8: Sustaining Positivity for Long-Term Growth

Creating Personal Affirmations and Mantras

In the journey towards personal growth and success, the power of positive thinking cannot be underestimated. Our thoughts shape our reality, and by harnessing the potential of affirmations and mantras, we can cultivate a more positive mindset and attract abundance into our lives.

Affirmations are positive statements that we repeat to ourselves, often in the present tense, to reinforce positive beliefs and overcome negative self-talk. They serve as a daily reminder of our capabilities and help us reprogram our subconscious mind. By consistently affirming our desired outcomes, we can align our thoughts with our goals and manifest them into reality.

To create personal affirmations, start by identifying areas of your life that you want to improve or beliefs you want to reinforce. Whether it's career success, relationships, health, or personal development, choose specific areas that matter most to you. Then, frame your affirmations in a positive, empowering manner. For example, if you want to enhance your self-confidence, your affirmation could be "I am confident and capable in all that I do."

Mantras, on the other hand, are short phrases or words that are repeated during meditation or daily life to focus the mind and cultivate positive energy. They can be used to anchor ourselves in the present moment, boost our mood, or shift our mindset. Mantras can be simple yet powerful tools for self-transformation.

When creating personal mantras, consider your current emotional state or the qualities you want to embody. It could be something like "I am calm and centered" or "I am open to infinite possibilities." Experiment with different mantras and choose the ones that resonate with you on a deeper level. Repeat them regularly, especially during moments of stress or self-doubt, to bring yourself back to a state of positivity and clarity.

Remember, the key to creating effective affirmations and mantras lies in repetition and belief. Consistently repeat them with conviction and visualize the desired outcome as if it has already happened. Embrace the positive emotions associated with your affirmations and mantras, and trust that the universe will conspire to bring your desires to fruition.

By integrating personal affirmations and mantras into your daily routine, you can rewire your subconscious mind and cultivate a positive mindset. Embrace the power of positive thinking and watch as it transforms every aspect of your life, leading you towards growth and success.

Building a Supportive Network

In the journey of life, it is essential to have a supportive network that uplifts and encourages us to reach our full potential. Surrounding ourselves with positive-minded individuals can have a profound impact on our overall well-being and success. This subchapter explores the significance of building a supportive network and provides practical strategies to nurture such relationships.

A supportive network consists of people who genuinely care about our growth and success. These individuals not only celebrate our achievements but also offer guidance and support during challenging times. Positive thinking is the key to attracting such individuals into our lives. When we cultivate a positive mindset, we become magnets for like-minded people who share our values and aspirations.

One of the first steps in building a supportive network is to identify the qualities we seek in our relationships. Are we looking for mentors who can guide us on our career path? Do we need friends who inspire us to maintain a positive attitude? By defining our needs, we can actively seek out individuals who possess these qualities and make a conscious effort to connect with them.

Networking events, social gatherings, and online communities focused on positive thinking are ideal platforms to meet like-minded individuals. Participating in these activities allows us to expand our social circle and build relationships based on shared interests and values. It is important to be open-minded and approachable, as this will attract potential supporters who resonate with our positive energy.

Another crucial aspect of building a supportive network is reciprocity. Support should be a two-way street, where we offer our assistance and encouragement to others as well. By being a positive influence in the lives of others, we create a ripple effect of positivity that strengthens our network and enhances our own personal growth.

Furthermore, maintaining regular communication and nurturing relationships is vital in building a supportive network. Regular check-ins, meaningful conversations, and providing support when needed foster deeper connections and create a sense of trust among individuals. It is through these connections that we find the strength and motivation to persevere during challenging times.

In conclusion, building a supportive network is an essential component of personal growth and success. Surrounding ourselves with positive-minded individuals who share our values and aspirations can have a profound impact on our overall well-being. By actively seeking out like-minded individuals, participating in networking events, and practicing reciprocity, we can build a strong and uplifting support system that propels us towards a life of fulfillment and achievement.

Practicing Self-Reflection and Self-Celebration

In the pursuit of leading a fulfilling and successful life, it is crucial to cultivate a habit of self-reflection and self-celebration. This subchapter focuses on the power of positive thinking and how it can contribute to personal growth and overall well-being. Whether you are a seasoned optimist or someone who wants to adopt a more positive mindset, this chapter provides practical strategies and insights to help you nurture positivity in every aspect of your life.

Self-reflection is the key to understanding ourselves better and gaining valuable insights into our thoughts, emotions, and actions. Taking the time to pause, evaluate, and contemplate our experiences allows us to develop self-awareness and identify areas for improvement. By engaging in self-reflection, we can celebrate our accomplishments, acknowledge our strengths, and identify areas where we need to grow.

One powerful technique for self-reflection is journaling. Writing down your thoughts, feelings, and experiences can provide clarity and perspective. It allows you to see patterns, identify recurring negative thoughts, and develop a more positive mindset. Regular journaling also enables you to track your progress, celebrate milestones, and learn from setbacks.

In addition to self-reflection, self-celebration plays a vital role in nurturing positivity. Often, we tend to focus on our shortcomings and failures, overlooking our achievements and successes. By acknowledging and celebrating our accomplishments, no matter how small, we can boost our self-confidence and cultivate a positive self-image.

Practicing self-celebration involves recognizing your accomplishments, expressing gratitude for your strengths, and rewarding yourself for your efforts. This could be as simple as treating yourself to something you enjoy, sharing your achievements with loved ones, or taking a moment to appreciate your growth journey.

Furthermore, surrounding yourself with positivity is essential in maintaining a positive mindset. Seek out like-minded individuals who uplift and inspire you. Engage in activities that bring you joy and fulfillment. Consciously choose to focus on the positive aspects of your life, even in challenging times.

Remember, positive thinking is not about denying or ignoring negative emotions or experiences. It is about acknowledging them, learning from them, and choosing to focus on the positive aspects of life.

In conclusion, self-reflection and self-celebration are essential practices for nurturing positivity in every aspect of life. By engaging in self-reflection, celebrating our accomplishments, and surrounding ourselves with positivity, we can cultivate a positive mindset and unlock our full potential. Embrace the power of positive thinking and watch as it transforms your life for the better.

Embracing a Lifetime Commitment to Positivity

In today's fast-paced and often challenging world, maintaining a positive mindset is essential for overall well-being and success. The power of positive thinking has been widely recognized, and countless individuals have experienced the transformative effects it can have on their lives. This subchapter, titled "Embracing a Lifetime Commitment to Positivity," aims to guide readers towards nurturing a lifelong dedication to cultivating positive thoughts and attitudes.

Positivity is not a fleeting emotion or a temporary state of mind; it is a way of life. It requires a conscious decision to approach every situation with optimism, resilience, and an unwavering belief in one's abilities. This commitment to positivity empowers individuals to overcome obstacles, build strong relationships, and achieve their goals.

To embark on this journey, it is crucial to understand the science behind positive thinking. Numerous studies have demonstrated the link between positive thoughts and improved mental and physical health. By consciously focusing on the positive aspects of life, individuals can reduce stress, increase happiness levels, and enhance overall well-being.

However, embracing a lifetime commitment to positivity goes beyond simply acknowledging its benefits. It requires consistent practice and the development of healthy habits. This subchapter will delve into various strategies and techniques that can be incorporated into daily life to foster a positive mindset.

One key aspect is gratitude – the practice of expressing appreciation for the blessings in our lives. By acknowledging and being thankful for even the smallest things, we cultivate an attitude of abundance and contentment. Additionally, cultivating self-compassion and promoting positive self-talk can help combat negative self-perceptions and boost self-confidence.

Furthermore, surrounding oneself with positive influences and like-minded individuals is paramount. Building a support network of individuals who share similar values and goals creates an environment that fosters growth and reinforces positive thinking.

While challenges and setbacks are inevitable, embracing a lifetime commitment to positivity enables individuals to view them as opportunities for growth and learning. By reframing negative experiences and focusing on the lessons they offer, individuals can bounce back stronger than ever.

In conclusion, "Embracing a Lifetime Commitment to Positivity" serves as a guide for individuals seeking to transform their lives through positive thinking. By adopting a positive mindset and incorporating various strategies into their daily lives, readers can nurture personal growth, build resilience, and ultimately achieve success in every aspect of life. This subchapter aims to inspire and empower individuals from all walks of life to embark on this transformative journey of embracing positivity, unlocking their true potential, and living a fulfilling and abundant life.

Conclusion: The Journey to Nurturing Growth and Success

In this final subchapter of "The Positivity Project: Nurturing Growth and Success in Every Aspect of Life," we come to the end of our transformative journey towards embracing positive thinking and cultivating a life filled with personal and professional success. Throughout this book, we have explored the power of positivity and its profound impact on every aspect of our lives. Now, it's time to reflect on our journey and understand how to continue nurturing growth and achieving success.

Positive thinking is not just a fleeting state of mind; it is a way of life. It requires consistent effort and a commitment to self-improvement. We have learned that positive thinking is not about ignoring challenges or denying negative emotions, but rather about embracing them and finding constructive ways to overcome them. By adopting a positive mindset, we can reframe setbacks as opportunities for growth, find solutions to problems, and build resilience.

One of the key takeaways from this book is the importance of self-belief. We have discovered that our thoughts shape our reality, and by believing in ourselves and our abilities, we can achieve remarkable things. By cultivating self-compassion and practicing self-care, we lay a solid foundation for personal growth. Through daily affirmations and visualizations, we can reinforce our positive beliefs and manifest our dreams into reality.

Another essential aspect of nurturing growth and success is the power of gratitude. By practicing gratitude, we shift our focus from what is lacking in our lives to what we already have. This shift in perspective opens up a world of possibilities and attracts more positive experiences. Gratitude also strengthens our relationships, enhances our overall well-being, and enables us to build a supportive community around us.

As we conclude this book, it is important to remember that the journey towards growth and success is ongoing. Each day presents new opportunities for growth and learning. By staying committed to our positive mindset, practicing self-love and gratitude, and surrounding ourselves with like-minded individuals, we can continue to nurture our personal and professional success.

Remember, it is not always about the destination; it is about the journey. Embrace each step with enthusiasm, knowing that every moment is an opportunity for growth. So, dear reader, as you embark on this wonderful adventure of nurturing growth and success, may you find joy, fulfillment, and abundance in every aspect of your life.

Wishing you a life filled with positivity and success!

www.ingramcontent.com/pod-product-compliance
Lightning Source LLC
LaVergne TN
LVHW052002060526
838201LV00059B/3800